Urn & Drum

Lila Matsumoto

Urn & Drum

Shearsman Books

First published in the United Kingdom in 2018 by
Shearsman Books
50 Westons Hill Drive
Emersons Green
BRISTOL
BS16 7DF

Shearsman Books Ltd Registered Office
30–31 St. James Place, Mangotsfield, Bristol BS16 9JB
(this address not for correspondence)

www.shearsman.com

ISBN 978-1-84861-568-7

The images in the section 'happy work' were provided by the
Wellcome Library, London, from their collection. Their assistance
is gratefully acknowledged.

Some of these poems first appeared in the following magazines/
publications: *A glimpse of, Archive of the Now, DATABLEED, Dusie,
Internal Leg and Cutlery Preview, Litmus, Rivet, SCREE,* and *Zarf.
Allegories from my Kitchen* was published as a chapbook by Sad
Press in 2015; *Soft Troika* was published as a chapbook by If a Leaf
Falls Press in 2016. Thank you to the editors of these magazines
and presses for their support.

Contents

For Matthew

happy work

born in flames

This upbeat, glitzy sleight of hand
is what I call stump work
or a battle cry

What I want to do – my desire of desires –
is to make a show about a stubborn individual
with an acute awareness of price and passion
dissatisfied with the pabulum of her lot

I would like it to be seen by the widest possible cross-section
        of people:
those who sing, those who don't, etc.

I will tell my critics, don't indulge yourselves in ex-cathedra
        judgments
and give them my best wishes
for several more centuries of women's work

ivory diagnostic figure, reclining

I often have the feeling I am in bed
rather than being an object
Monday to Friday, I escape the narrowness and permanence
of definition

The world which surrounds me
is constantly catalyzed by personalities
whose lives are driven forward
by the spirit of automation

You can see that there is something alive
or operating
in me

Through my body I attempt to treat myself
as an equivalent and independent element

This may be in vain I know
but I believe dreams clothe the mind
and I am thankful we have use for costumes

practical style

A long time coming, this pre-natal story.

When we first started out we had a more timid approach
but we began to realise that there was this thing

Well, it didn't even have a name then
but what you can call an out-of-body state
where you become interested in the small changes
your own hands can make

I was twenty-one when I first came to this city
I thought to myself, this is where I want to be

We were fascinated by the activities we saw
It gave us many ideas about how we could take our materials
and splice, cut, and paste them

Over eight years and an abundance of work
we have experimented with all aspects of soft, moist matter
People say we are a kind of ropy orchestra
that would make any singing saloon jealous

body advocate

When you were clapping your hands, I fell into a trance
a rock star or go-go dancer or were you shelving objects

I fell into your repetition

First a gesture then a demonstration
then a response, then an alien
smarting to the air

Your gaze was definitely neutral
You seemed to be interested in reflecting something back

To me it seemed like happy work
like the gradual lengthening of torso
and legs

world of sporting chance

The question I get the most is, how did we do it?

All I know is, there was a grid on the floor in our minds and
each person got carried through their designated square

We communicated about how to move that person from their
square to the next person's square
We were workers moving lumber and that's how it felt to do
that action

"blood" or "tears of the tree"
I don't know what had more weight to it

noise dirge

Misery, or not –

it's an intense relationship
on my side of the wall
I'm trying to listen with big ears
to the light that's shining to itself

Signs are transmitted to me
I take notice of them
Then I add and omit notes
and it sounds better to me this way

tiny content: hol-li - ho-li - day. brave ho – li – day

Allegories from my Kitchen

Morning

The morning is sticky yellow and gray. I reach into my boxy and what do I find there – soxy. The frequent cat sits outside the window and peers in and in. I dislike its sensuous lips all over again. The kettle is in a huff and the eggs griddle griddle. A small and mad insect circles the coffee jar lid. Pinching the plates between pinky and thumb I dip them one by one into the water which undulates with fresh promise. Life is a kind of theatre where the characters sing or dance most or all of the time.

Peaches

Six peaches in a box, cradled by fleshy foam sleeves. Extricating the fruits from their holders, I place them hastily in a bowl. What do you want to do? I ask the six foams, now unburdened of their charges. I gesture to the whole wide world. But I know that their destiny had been wholly shaped by their capabilities. The key is not at home in the lock, it is imprisoned in it. And as the key was made for the lock, the foam had been made for the peach, and now peachless, they lie there numb and insignificant.

Pancake

Oh! The *horror vacui* of the crevice between refrigerator and wall. I call my reliable caulker, and she arrives after lunchtime with an armful of smooshable foodstuffs, eventually electing pancakes as her most preferred medium.

Chicken

I invite over C., with whom I've been experiencing considerable misunderstandings. It seemed to me — though I confess to being prone to dramatic analogies — that we had fallen into a cold and inhospitable well where the luminous circle of kinship is but a distant vision.

I say to C., let's pretend to be toddler twins placed suddenly in the driver's seat of a train making its way up the Hudson River Valley. Alright, C. says. We voice the stops at the approach, attempting unison, watching each other's mouths carefully to see when the tongue would hit the palate. But due to the stubborn paces of our speaking, unaccustomed to such forced twinning, the destinations are never synchronized and come out as ghostly echoes of each intention. Yonkers - Ossining - Garrison - Cold Spring. At Poughkeepsie we disembark for food at Janet's Chicken Shack, ordering a takeaway with a few extra forks.

Evening arrives, and the wind feels unexpectedly clean on my skin. The purpling hills tickle the trains rattling gladly home: Eh- oh eh-oh. Then the mist arrives, making itself comfortable in the riverbank. Listening to the distant revving of the motorcycles on the highway, I am suddenly punctured by sadness. Our food grows cold. So this is your past, C. says, making three-dotted perforations on the chicken skin surface. One part, I say bravely, and place the chicken into the resuscitation oven.

Pickles / Jam

Is this feudal? Me brining your foods. In the dream I licked the interior of your computer with broad concern. I want to make sincere pickles and for this reason all of those carrots *will* be exfoliated. I can assure you that with cynical friends I am no happier, just more swayed by arguments for the contrary situation jam band.

Fondant Cake

This fondant cake is here for you. A crisp, almost brittle crust, and a rich and dark crumb. Also this grief bacon.

Radio

Following the reporting of a news item that made him chuckle, the radio presenter adjusts his bathos to say that a baby has fallen out of an eleventh floor window, but has survived with minor injuries. He only changed mode, H. says, to create the dramatic tension of the dead baby and the alive baby. Yes, V. says, the presenter is an auteur, he wants to stiffen us in order to relax us. The baby survived because it is cushy, K. says. The baby unlike the listener has no expectations. It never stiffens itself. When it fell it was loose and its looseness saved it. I moisten the tip of my baguette with melted ice-water from my cup.

Landish

Princess of flexible bamboo scattering light

Resisting the gloss of love's wide-eyed lens
scooping deep into my self-help muesli
I know I must change my life or 'otherwise perish'
Why does nearly every evening summon us to feelings
in the hanging gardens of late scepticism
Maltha, gilsonite and bitumen encircle
the mountainous situation of my innerscape
Olive, oak, tamarish, juniper and bamboo
the flowering, perennial evergreen of my namesake
See me as bull, or ram, as man, or mollusc
or I must become my own angleworm and fish myself silly

Bird sense

i.

naked together among the hoods,
the songbirds give a brief history of luck
and how to read graveyards

the hungry city is a diary
of dog-walkers and feral timid souls.
rousseau was wrong

what it means to be human
is to gossip from the forest
of a silent state

ii.

manage your mammoth
office politics.
what has nature ever done for us

but eat & run.
an examined life bears witness
to living and thinking sound asleep.

in the hour between dog and wolf
are you smart enough
to work for google

iii.

walking home, the fish
in my ear kills the middle-class dream
of britain's heritage pubs

war is dead long live war
and seven deadly sins.
the theory that would not die

rambles on
and beauties in the beast
run wild

Beavers of Alloa

Look about ye... The wee county
                — Mottos of Clackmannanshire historic county

More than you imagined,
you will see small trees
and branches cut to a pencil point.

Through the scribbled woods,
a tower.
No not a tower,
it's too squat.
More like a keep.
But says we're right on it.
Ok the other tower
across the roundabout.
Ring the illuminated lion growl.

Ok – I see a familiar eyebrow
squiggle through the arrowslit.
& the familiar gleam of buttock
in the garderobe
from where my lover's pet moths flutter
wings imprinted with sparrowfart.
She wears a strange scowl,
gives a cruel yank.

What luxurious barbarity
is in this home of Lord Kames,
farmer-philosopher!
Few creatures can effect
such profound positive changes
to the environment as he.

Watch him don the un-beaver mask
and direct the moss-lairds to strip
peat from the floodplain & float
them downstream,
those furry parcels made in earthbelly.

We can exchange now
cultural methodologies
on equivalent basis free
from impediment
so smooth
like a roundabout
& vehicles are minnows in fishpools
at the top of the latest mogul's regent's tower.

Meanwhile, the real beavers.
They loiter bellyout.
With no watery coppice to trim to saw
& where no salmonid parr tarry.

Little big one

after Philip Maltman's painting, Little Big One

low rain

weather depression

fifth to root for chorus

third to root for verse

if you liked it you should have put a ring on it

you should have en-sphered it

imagine: the grey is the hardware for the wire heart.

avant-garde Hindu position

man stands as tree

woman sits off as woodpecker

feather   father

withdrawal of the first completer

and the mechanism of the bloodline

which made the pattern

who made the wall and the white nest's eye

The Levels of Cognizance

Seeing things

Conceive our eyes to the ledge.
Join the six to seven million cohorts
of high mystery, beguilers
of all carnal stenographers.
So the tyranny of radiant vision leans back
bathing in vivid, historical dreams.
(the books moss over and over)

Knowing things

What, finally, do we elongate ourselves for?
A swoonier, more sublime eraser?
Or a more gullible history,
longing to loosen wonky heirs and voluptuous deficits?

Hearing things

Stirred melted yielding
orifice always open for business
invasion by unspeakable
loss + bliss

Feeling things

Not in ideas but in feelings

Believing things

'text itself'
'psychic needs'
'art and culture'
'beauty'
'the other'
'mia farrow'
'standing back'
'hairlines'
'knowingness'
'I'
'books'
'style'
'style'

Temple

Where I am
someone is there
in the dark

> To belong to the word "write"
> I had to not understand
> nor question myself the light desire
> that attracts my gaze

like an avid moment disrupting
the often said
knowing just imperious power

Nonnet for checked king

Betrayed or avenged, sadness is the condition of the king
— Gillian Rose

In my hurt, I resume with such heart
to go home. Outside the wild mind:
evening's keening. Defences
fail, as colours, the leaves.
A bughouse game this
is. Incomplete
again. Dine
again,
wait.

Meteor

Is it only interested
in following form,
is that its solitary concern.

If there is it and me
do I initiate the form of encounter.
                    I don't mind

But after all this, the delirium
of contact set to un-casual music,
is it up to me now to articulate
what I think is its shape
and velocity.

To what extent is it sustained by longing.
To what extent is that longing mine. It's better I'm better it's
better. If the fluctuations come closer
and closer together –

is that important or not important to its present position.

inclined plane

something of this view

                engaged in.

  silence

              contrary object

                                    love

is it true?

      does it nest

                for seven days

           then hauled away

                  they are right

                      we must have been

too improvident –

                              nothing
                    was tucked into a corner

          for later.

          the aeroplanes
                         write our dream

once in a while

                              & carrying mail never did

require war,

                the traces

                              being too shy.

                         was subordination
          to duty

                              otherwise

Landish

You read in the news that the weird sisters are no longer subsidised by the charity commission. We must now work overtime to patrol the gates of hades, and ensure the two-headed dog, you forget its name, is fed four times a day, or is it twice, two feeds per head. Lest the unhappy from unhappy foreign places, they who have unusually strong powers of flight, jungle into a swarm and knit us all in a complicity of shame and trouble.

♒

Is the standing stone worth the skirting by the plough? Should the doses of anxious attention we administer, wittingly or unwittingly, be up for an annual review? A white sheet escapes the clothing line and streaks across the field. You have never seen such a joyful thing.

♒

I'll do anything for my baby fig tree. If it presses its hands forlornly against the window pane, wanting to join the yellows and pinks, I'll tear down the whole house with my ungainly hammer. It's true what you've heard, we let our animus run riot. We let our soapbox become a prostate and play golf in yards of unmitigated sun. We boil owl pellets with impunity and insert fingers in sides of rotten fruit and really rummage around in there.

〰〰

Roll on john, or jack, or any of you tow-headed boys – fall back down to earth on your air break outside aztec softplay. Toss your cares over the transom into mother big river, turn the sun's bright wheel, select all, rename all, in our garden trum trum, in our garden foresaken, rogue russet's symphony, september tomato's diluvian dream, the blight and the gooseberry fool and song of the oyamel.

Got to Get Your Love

tizzy steals an airbag from a truck
rocking
a spike with a mullet

my project packing nada
I shave your name into my skull
get hit with an egg or a jar   ships
into unthought known

there but for the grace of no bobby
I'm a bush   a bush   a bush

no she didn't edit   //   dope
congas and claps eggs on

flame retardants   in her pants

kitsch

satchel's page   //   strikeout

whence
the terminator tells the entire kitchen staff to gather around

who's *he* to say? to tell us to do a stupid dance

<< instrumental for bashful >>

nevertheless

I acknowledge your rucksack following
and the use of the obsession with sex
as a weapon against spiritual bankruptcy

I fill many uncertain breeches
with all kinds of cheesy comestibles

cheesy but not insurmountable

maybe an ego echo

She hosted the hell out of that tapas party!
even though we saw straight through her lie
whalebone on the mantel piece
not really from colonsay

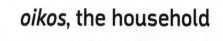

oikos, the household

Flask

Looking at my tail, smiling all the while. Renegade beginning attracts jealousy, casual assurance, and eventually, abduction. Crack my ribs, ring all my days into marble.

Pair of cups

Twenty candied discs newly opened, pinwheels to sunflowers.
First outlined in coal blue. Contending reds dovetail so
neatly.

Jar

Nothing more than a worry humped into wood. But note its lightness, a contradiction to gravity's will. Because the mottled back and collapsed shoulder is evidence of a grievance.

Jar II

A thought jostles for attention, fronds alarmingly when poked. Scurrying fishes circle two times around. To not mention it is to delete it, to mention it is to advertise its wares.

Mug

A song is quiet, is square. Or is tight-capped to landscape's skull. Leaning flowers carpet thickly, a speculation of bulbs and serrated grass.

Cope

Not animated by the wind, dove deeply into one pond.
The rebel merged in the image of its master. Cross-hatched,
clobbered yellow, with wild hair running down the road.

Sugar bowl

To support the one eating grapes on the turquoise-rimmed
dias...

Teapot

This is what happens when you stop paying attention. A hand grasps a neck grasps a parrot's legs. Who is holding whom captive?

Jug

A silver reason hammered by a chasing punch. It was borne from hesitance; it is a want despite the lack.

Vase

Moving past the gate, a slow shape unfolds: seven pearls escape from a flute and settle into the crook of a scythe. By the rigid trellis, suspended birds once cascaded, met.

Soft Troika

Wherever there are hands, on peace-splayed cloth or on two blue bands holding strong, holding side-snake. Attenuated fingers follow skirt's striation, raiding the leaf-shaped hem. Or raiding for the purposes of urn and drum. Grasping the backs of chairs and scrolls of music, clenching a hat or a bent croquet mallet. Guiding a child's feet into a basin, pinching a sponge, unable to tame a wild and unkempt brood. Gesturing an invitation to be merry, gripping a forked stick to lift hay down. Or as entreaty, pointing to heel in lean supplication. A soft troika of pen, coin, and jug.

Follow the everyday without privileging adoresome buildings. Humble and banal objects are ciphers in whose gridded pink lens correspondences speak in fugues. You can know them in their lean, in which the rituals of dayspring are constructed. In this view, things are cemeteries where significance is buried. Objects aren't torpid. Like the cry of the cat, they're strange machines, continually evolving from day to night, and back again.

Plique-à-jour, letting in sunlight. I stood there every day for four months, knowing there was a high failure rate. I had temporary backup, but fired most of them, and the others were chased away by acid rain. In the glass is an icon blinking for action. There is a ripple sometimes, a surface tension. I think it's being used by a king, in a luxury house, and he's keen for it not to be disturbed or copied. This example looks quite rare, extremely fragile, like the eight pinnacle points on the crown of some eleventh-century saint.

Being in your body is like … a gently discombobulating dream, taken out of the air like a song subject to more or less instant improvisation by other singers who rewrite the tune when they get it. But you may say I exaggerate. You may say, it's more like a dandelion's downy seed stealthily floating, poker-faced, an angel's right hook. Well, some days your motility seems to me a strange thing. I remind myself constantly that your ridges allow for increased leverage when picking up objects or walking barefoot.

Over time, a small cult came to form around her cascade of shrubberies: both by the weirdos already hip to her outlandish flowerpits, and the ones whose horizons were being bagged with every slip of geranium. At the present moment, it's hard to believe that we will ever be at a point in history when mountain floras were underrepresented, especially in the softer light of dungeons.

This is a project helmed by two friends who live in a cul-de-sac, produced by one of their dads who's probably best known for his work with the sprawl collective Loose Liver. Their sound can be likened to high-definition hay: seemingly prosaic, but makes you look twice because it gives off a ridiculous amount of bloom! In fact, the best part may be the tacet section, when (presumably) one of their friends walks into the studio and says something about a 'celery bandage'. But it seems tangential to focus on that particular detail.

'High jinks in the cathedral'. Circa 1908, cotton, grain, stone, ink. The shadow of a particularly overawed beast hangs over it, calling attention to the texture, rather than the specularity, of the work. When one thinks of voluptuaries, they naturally think of multilayer soul gems, astrakhan collars, and snails fattened on milk. One could also throw in, for instance, circulets, silver crockery, bejewelled hand carts, and small baskets woven from rare rushes.

I often wonder where you can get your hands on those hats worn by Enlightenment philosophers as seen in their portraits. Do you know the ones I mean – they look like fezzes but are more squat, more turban-like, softer-looking. They usually come in a velveteen or satin trim and for this reason sybarites often wear them. I can't even begin to search for these hats, not knowing what they are called.

Printed in September 2022
by Rotomail Italia S.p.A., Vignate (MI) - Italy